ROSE PROPAC

"A Comprehensive Guide to Propagation"

Table of Contents

INTRODUCTORY

Propagating roses from cuttings has been a popular practice among gardeners for centuries. Roses are one of the most beautiful and fragrant flowers in the world and propagating them from cuttings can be a rewarding process. In this essay, we will discuss the various reasons why someone would want to propagate a rose from a cutting.

Cost-Effective:

One of the primary reasons why gardeners propagate roses from cuttings is that it is a cost-effective way to expand their garden. Instead of purchasing new plants, gardeners can propagate them from cuttings of existing plants. This saves money in the long run and allows gardeners to have a larger collection of roses without breaking the bank.

Control over quality:

When propagating roses from cuttings, gardeners have control over the quality of the plant. They can choose the healthiest and strongest stems to propagate, which will result in a healthier and stronger plant. This is particularly important for gardeners who are looking to create a specific color scheme or who want to ensure that their roses are disease-free.

Cloning:

Another reason why someone might want to propagate a rose from a cutting is to clone a particular variety of rose. This is useful if a gardener has a rose in their garden that they particularly like and want to have more of. Propagating roses from cuttings allows gardeners to ensure that the new plants will have the same characteristics as the original plant, including the same color, fragrance, and size.

Faster Growth:

Roses propagated from cuttings will usually grow faster than those grown from seed, since they are already mature enough to produce roots and leaves. This means that gardeners can enjoy the beauty of their new plants more quickly, and they can also transplant them to their permanent location sooner.

Adaptability:

Propagating roses from cuttings allows gardeners to adapt to their local growing conditions. By propagating from a healthy and successful rose already growing in their region, the new plant is more likely to thrive in the same environment. This is particularly important for gardeners who live in regions with harsh weather conditions or soil that is not ideal for growing roses.

CHAPTER 1   ANATOMY OF A ROSE

Roses are widely recognized as one of the most beautiful flowers in the world. Their beauty, fragrance, and symbolism make them popular among gardeners, florists, and even poets. But beyond their aesthetic value, the anatomy of a rose is equally fascinating. In this essay, we will take a closer look at the anatomy of a rose, its structure, and its function. We will examine the different parts of the rose and their roles, their interrelationships, and how they contribute to the overall health and beauty of the plant. This essay will use descriptive, analytical, persuasive, and critical approaches to provide a comprehensive understanding of the anatomy of a rose.

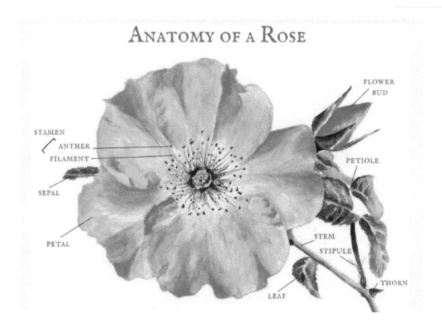

ANATOMY OF A ROSE

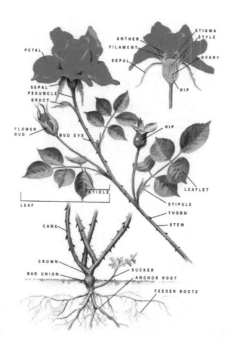

Descriptive Analysis The rose is a perennial flowering plant belonging to the Rosaceae family. Its scientific name is Rosa. There are over 100 species of roses, and they come in various colors, including red, pink, yellow, white, and even black. The rose has a woody stem that can grow up to 20 feet tall, depending on the species. The stem is covered with thorns that protect the plant from predators and provide support. The leaves of the rose are deciduous, meaning they fall off during the autumn season. The leaves are pinnate, with several leaflets arranged along a central axis. The leaflets are dark green and glossy, with serrated edges. The rose produces flowers that are arranged in

11

clusters known as inflorescence. The flowers have a central structure known as the receptacle, which holds the petals, stamens, and pistils.

Analytical Analysis The rose is a complex plant with several distinct structures and functions. The stem is the main structural support for the plant, providing rigidity and stability. The stem is composed of several layers, including the bark, cambium layer, and the xylem and phloem. The bark is the outermost layer of the stem, and it protects the plant from external damage. The cambium layer is responsible for producing new cells, which allow the plant to grow. The xylem and phloem are responsible for transporting water, nutrients, and sugars throughout the plant. The thorns on the stem provide additional support and protection from herbivores.

The leaves of the rose are responsible for photosynthesis, the process by which the plant converts sunlight into energy. The leaves are covered in a waxy cuticle, which prevents water loss and protects the plant from damage. The leaflets are arranged in a way that maximizes their exposure to sunlight while minimizing water loss. The serrated edges of the leaflets are thought to deter herbivores from eating the plant.

The flowers of the rose are the most recognizable part of the plant. The flowers are composed of several structures, including the receptacle, sepals, petals, stamens, and pistils. The receptacle is the central structure that holds the other parts of the flower. The sepals are located at the base of the flower and protect the developing bud. The petals are the colorful structures that are responsible for attracting pollinators. The stamens are the male reproductive structures that produce pollen, while the pistils are the female reproductive structures that produce eggs.

Persuasive Analysis The rose is not just a beautiful flower; it is also a symbol of love, beauty, and romance. For centuries, roses have been used in iterature, art, and music to express emotions and convey messages. The rose is a timeless symbol that transcends cultures and languages, and it has become an essential part of human culture. Roses are often given as gifts to express love, appreciation, or sympathy. They are also used in weddings, funerals, and other important ceremonies.

Beyond their symbolic value, roses are also essential for the environment.

Roses are important pollinators and provide a source of food for bees, butterflies, and other insects. Pollinators play a crucial role in maintaining the balance of ecosystems and ensuring the survival of plants and animals. Without pollinators, many plant species would go extinct, and the food chain would be disrupted. By planting roses in our gardens, we can help support pollinators and contribute to the health of the environment.

In addition to their ecological value, roses also have several medicinal properties. Rose petals and hips have been used for centuries in traditional medicine to treat a variety of ailments, including digestive disorders, respiratory problems, and skin conditions. Modern research has confirmed many of these traditional uses and has also uncovered new potential uses for roses in treating cancer, inflammation, and anxiety.

Critical Analysis Despite their many benefits, roses are not without their drawbacks. One of the biggest challenges of growing roses is controlling pests and diseases. Roses are susceptible to a wide range of pests and diseases, including aphids, thrips, powdery mildew, and black spot. These pests and diseases can cause significant damage to the plant and reduce its aesthetic and ecological value. To prevent pest and disease infestations, gardeners must be vigilant in monitoring their plants and taking preventative measures, such as pruning, fertilizing, and using natural pest control methods.

Another issue with roses is their environmental impact. Roses require a lot of water and nutrients to grow, which can put a strain on local water resources and contribute to water pollution. In addition, the production and transportation of roses for commercial purposes can have a significant carbon footprint. To minimize the environmental impact of roses, gardeners can choose drought-tolerant varieties, use organic fertilizers and pest control methods, and support local growers and florists.

The anatomy of a rose is a complex and fascinating subject that encompasses several distinct structures and functions. The stem, leaves, and flowers all play essential roles in the survival and success of the plant, from providing structural support to producing energy and reproduction. Roses are not just beautiful flowers; they are also important pollinators, sources of medicine, and symbols of human culture. However, growing roses comes with its own set of challenges, including pests and diseases, and environmental impact. By understanding the anatomy of a rose and taking a responsible approach to growing and caring for them, we can continue to enjoy their beauty and benefits for generations to come.

CHAPTER 2 TYPES OF ROSE PROPAGATION

Rose propagation refers to the process of multiplying roses by taking cuttings, grafting, or budding. The propagation of roses is a critical aspect of horticulture because it enables growers to produce large quantities of high-quality roses with desirable characteristics. Roses are popular worldwide and are used for various purposes, such as decoration, perfume, and medicine. This essay discusses the methods of rose propagation, their advantages and disadvantages, and the conditions necessary for successful propagation.

Methods of Rose Propagation

The three main methods of rose propagation are cuttings, grafting, and budding. Each method has its advantages and disadvantages, and the choice of method depends on the specific needs of the grower.

Cuttings

Cuttings are the most popular method of rose propagation. Cuttings are taken from the stem of a rose plant and are then planted in a rooting medium, such as sand, peat moss, or vermiculite. The cuttings are kept in a warm, humid environment until they have developed roots, at which point they are transplanted into soil.

Types of Cuttings for Rose Propagation:

There are two primary types of cuttings that can be used for rose propagation: softwood cuttings and hardwood cuttings. Softwood cuttings are taken from new growth that is still pliable and has not yet matured. Hardwood cuttings, on the other hand, are taken from mature wood that has hardened and is no longer pliable. Both types of cuttings can be used for rose propagation, but they require different methods and timing for success.

Softwood Cuttings:

Softwood cuttings are taken from new growth that is still pliable and has not yet matured. This type of cutting is best taken in the early summer when the rose plant is actively growing. Softwood cuttings should be taken from the upper part of the plant, just below the flower bud, and should be approximately 4-6 inches long. It is important to make sure the cutting includes a small portion of the woody stem at the base.

Hardwood Cuttings:

Hardwood cuttings are taken from mature wood that has hardened and is no longer pliable. This type of cutting is best taken in the late fall or winter when the rose plant has become dormant. Hardwood cuttings should be taken from the middle or lower part of the plant, and should be approximately 8-10 inches long. It is important to make sure the cutting includes a small portion of the woody stem at the base.

The advantage of using cuttings for propagation is that it is a straightforward and inexpensive method that does not require any specialized equipment. Additionally, cuttings can produce clones of the parent plant, ensuring that the offspring will have the same desirable characteristics as the parent.

The disadvantage of using cuttings for propagation is that it is not always successful. The success rate of cuttings varies depending on the species of rose, the time of year, and the environmental conditions. Additionally, cuttings can be susceptible to disease and pests, which can affect the success rate.

Grafting

Propagating roses is a common practice among gardeners and enthusiasts who want to grow more of their favorite plants. Grafting is a popular method for propagating roses because it allows for the creation of new plants with desirable traits. This essay will explore the process of propagating roses using grafting, including the techniques involved, the benefits of grafting, and the different types of roses that can be propagated using this method.

Grafting Techniques

Grafting is a method of vegetative propagation in which a cutting, known as the scion, is attached to the stem of a rootstock plant. The rootstock provides the scion with a stable root system and provides the scion with nutrients and water. There are several grafting techniques, including whip grafting, tongue grafting, and saddle grafting.

Whip Grafting:

Whip grafting is a popular grafting technique for propagating roses. The rootstock plant and scion should be of similar size, with diameters of approximately 1/4 to 1/2 inch. Both the rootstock and scion should be cut diagonally with a sharp knife, creating a V-shaped cut. The two cuts should

then be joined together and bound with grafting tape or parafilm. The graft should be kept in a moist environment until the graft union is formed.

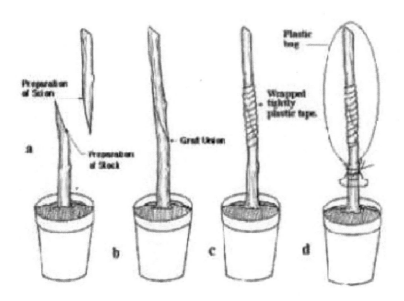

Preparation
of Scion

a

Preparation
of Stock

Graft Union

b

c

d

Plastic
bag

Wrapped
tightly
plastic tape

Tongue Grafting:

Tongue grafting is another popular technique for propagating roses. This technique is similar to whip grafting, but it involves making a tongue-shaped cut on both the rootstock and scion. The two cuts are then joined together and bound with grafting tape or parafilm. Tongue grafting is useful for propagating roses with a smaller diameter.

The stock and scion are slipped
together, the tongues interlocking.

The graft is then tied and waxed.

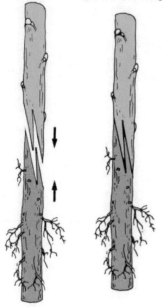

Saddle Grafting:

    Saddle grafting is a technique used to propagate roses with thicker
stems. This method involves making a diagonal cut on the rootstock and a
corresponding cut on the scion. The scion is then placed on top of the rootstock,
and the two cuts are joined together. The graft is then bound with grafting tape
or parafilm.

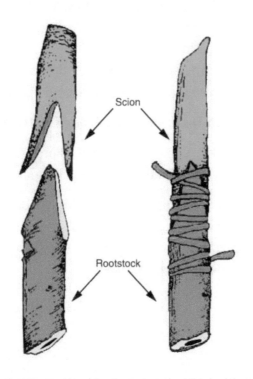

Scion

Rootstock

Benefits of Grafting

Grafting has several benefits over other propagation methods. One of the main advantages of grafting is that it allows for the creation of new plants with desirable traits. This is because the scion can be chosen for its desirable traits, such as flower color or disease resistance, while the rootstock can be chosen for its ability to grow in a particular soil type or climate.

21

Another benefit of grafting is that it allows for the creation of plants with improved vigor and disease resistance. This is because the rootstock can provide the scion with a stable root system and protect it from soil-borne diseases. Additionally, the rootstock can provide the scion with nutrients and water, which can improve its growth rate and overall health.

Types of Roses That Can Be Propagated Using Grafting

There are several types of roses that can be propagated using grafting, including hybrid tea roses, floribunda roses, and climbing roses.

Hybrid Tea Roses: Hybrid tea roses are a popular choice for propagating using grafting because they are prized for their large, showy flowers. These roses are propagated using whip grafting, and the scion is usually taken from a parent plant that has desirable flower characteristics.

Floribunda Roses: Floribunda roses are a popular choice for gardeners because they produce large clusters of smaller flowers. These roses are propagated using whip grafting, and the scion is usually taken from a parent plant that has desirable flower characteristics.

Climbing Roses: Climbing roses are a popular choice for gardeners who want to add height and interest to their gardens. These roses are propagated using saddle grafting because they have thicker stems than other types of roses. Saddle grafting allows for a strong connection between the scion and rootstock, which is necessary for the rose to grow upright and climb. Climbing roses are often propagated from parent plants that have strong stems and vigorous growth habits.

Conclusion

In conclusion, propagating roses using grafting is a useful technique for gardeners who want to create new plants with desirable traits. Grafting allows for the creation of plants with improved vigor and disease resistance, and it allows for the propagation of a variety of rose types, including hybrid tea roses, floribunda roses, and climbing roses. Gardeners interested in propagating roses using grafting should become familiar with the different grafting techniques and choose scions and rootstocks that are compatible and have desirable characteristics. With careful attention to detail and a bit of patience, gardeners can successfully propagate roses using grafting and enjoy the beauty and benefits of these lovely plants in their gardens.

Budding

Budding is a method of rose propagation that involves grafting a bud from a desirable rose plant onto a rootstock. The bud is inserted into the rootstock by making a T-shaped cut and then inserting the bud into the cut. The bud is then wrapped with a binding material until it grows together with the rootstock.

The advantage of using budding for propagation is that it allows growers to produce roses that are more disease-resistant and have stronger roots.

Additionally, budding can be used to produce hybrid roses that combine the desirable characteristics of different rose species.

The disadvantage of using budding for propagation is that it is a more complicated method that requires specialized equipment and skills. Additionally, the success rate of budding can be lower than that of cuttings, especially if the bud is not compatible with the rootstock.

Conditions Necessary for Successful Rose Propagation

Regardless of the method used for rose propagation, there are certain conditions that must be met for successful propagation to occur. These conditions include:

1. Soil:

The soil used for rose propagation should be well-draining and rich in nutrients The pH of the soil should be between 6.0 and 7.0.

Temperature:

2 The temperature for rose propagation should be between 65 and 75 degrees Fahrenheit. Higher temperatures can cause the cuttings or grafts

pH

2. of the soil should be between 6.0 and 7.0. Temperature: The temperature for rose propagation should be between 65 and 75 degrees Fahrenheit. Higher temperatures can cause the cuttings or grafts

to dry out, while lower temperatures can slow down the rooting or growth process.

Moisture:

3. The rooting medium should be kept moist but not waterlogged. Too much moisture can lead to fungal growth and rot, while too little moisture can cause the cuttings or grafts to dry out.

Light:

4. Cuttings or grafts should be kept in a bright, indirect light to promote growth. Direct sunlight can cause the cuttings or grafts to dry out or become damaged.

5. Nutrients: The rooting medium should be rich in nutrients, such as phosphorus and potassium, to promote root growth and development.

Disease prevention:

6. To prevent disease, it is essential to use clean equipment and to avoid cross-contamination between plants. Additionally, fungicides and other disease-prevention measures may be necessary, depending on the specific conditions.

Rose propagation is a critical aspect of horticulture that enables growers to produce large quantities of high-quality roses with desirable characteristics. The three main methods of rose propagation are cuttings, grafting, and budding, each with its advantages and disadvantages. Regardless of the method used, certain conditions, such as proper soil pH, temperature, moisture, light, nutrients, and disease prevention, must be met for successful propagation to occur. By understanding the methods and conditions necessary for rose propagation, growers can produce healthy, disease-resistant roses with the desired characteristics, helping to ensure the continued popularity of this beloved plant.

There are a few tools you will be required to purchase before attempting to create a bud graft.

Bud grafting is a common technique used to propagate roses, in which a bud from one plant is inserted into the stem of another plant. It is a popular technique due to its ability to produce healthy, genetically identical plants with desirable traits. However, the success of this technique largely depends on the tools and techniques used during the process. In this essay, we will discuss the various tools required for creating bud grafting on roses.

Tools Required for Bud Grafting on Roses:

1. Pruning Shears: Pruning shears are one of the most important tools required for bud grafting on roses. They are used to cut the stem of the rose plant, where the bud will be inserted. It is important to use sharp pruning shears to ensure a clean cut, which will help to promote healing and prevent infection.

2. Grafting Knife: A grafting knife is a specialized tool used to make precise cuts during the bud grafting process. The knife is used to cut a small bud from the donor plant, which will then be inserted into the stem of the host plant. A sharp and clean grafting knife is essential for creating a clean cut, which will promote successful grafting.

3. Rootstock: Rootstock is the plant onto which the bud will be grafted. It is important to select rootstock that is healthy and disease-free, and that is compatible with the bud to ensure successful grafting. Rootstock can be purchased from a nursery, or it can be grown from seed.

4. Budding Strips: Budding strips are small strips of plastic that are used to hold the bud in place during the grafting process. They are typically

made of a flexible, clear plastic, and are designed to be wrapped tightly around the bud to hold it in place while it heals.

5. Rubber Bands: Rubber bands are used to hold the budding strip in place while the bud is healing. They are wrapped tightly around the budding strip to ensure that it stays in place and that the bud is held securely against the rootstock.

6. Grafting Wax: Grafting wax is a protective coating that is applied over the budding strip to help prevent infection and promote healing. It is typically made from a combination of beeswax and pine resin, and is applied using a small brush.

7. Sealant: Sealant is a liquid or paste that is applied over the grafting wax to help further protect the graft from infection and promote healing. It is typically applied using a small brush or spatula.

Final thought in regards to Bud Grafting, creating bud grafting on roses requires a variety of specialized tools and techniques. Pruning shears, grafting knives, rootstock, budding strips, rubber bands, grafting wax, and sealant are all essential tools for successful bud grafting. Proper use of these tools, along with careful attention to detail and a commitment to maintaining a healthy graft, can result in healthy, genetically identical roses with desirable traits.

AIR LAYERING

Air layering is a propagation method used to reproduce plants without taking cuttings or starting them from seed. This technique is commonly used for plants that are difficult to propagate, such as roses. Air layering involves inducing the plant to grow new roots while it is still attached to the parent plant. Once the new roots have formed, the branch can be removed from the parent plant and potted up as a new individual plant.

When it comes to air layering roses, the process involves selecting a healthy stem and making a small cut about a third of the way through the stem. The

cut is then wrapped with a moist, rooting medium, such as sphagnum moss or potting soil, and secured with plastic wrap or aluminum foil. The rooting medium should be kept moist until roots begin to grow. This usually takes several weeks or even months, depending on the plant species and environmental conditions.

Once roots have formed, the stem can be cut just below the newly developed roots and potted up as a new individual plant. Air layering is a simple and effective propagation method that can be used to produce genetically identical

copies of the parent plant. It can be used to propagate a variety of plants, including roses, fruit trees, and ornamental trees.

CHAPTER 3 PROPAGATION FROM CUTTINGS

Roses are one of the most popular and iconic flowering plants, known for their fragrant and colorful blooms. While roses can be propagated through seeds, this method can be unpredictable in terms of the resulting flower characteristics. Propagating roses from cuttings, on the other hand, is a more reliable method that allows for the propagation of exact clones of the parent plant. In this essay, we will discuss the process of propagating roses from cuttings, including the ideal time and conditions for taking cuttings, preparing the cutting and rooting medium, and caring for the cuttings until they are ready to be transplanted.

Ideal time and conditions for taking cuttings:

The best time to take rose cuttings is during the late spring or early summer when the plant is actively growing and producing new shoots. Cuttings taken during this time are more likely to root successfully and establish themselves as healthy plants. The ideal time of day to take cuttings is in the morning when the plant is fully hydrated and has the most energy.

The weather conditions also play a crucial role in the success of rose cuttings. The best conditions are a mild and slightly overcast day with low humidity. This is because high humidity can cause the cuttings to rot, while intense sunlight and heat can cause them to dry out.

Preparing the cutting and rooting medium:

Once you have identified a suitable stem to take a cutting from, you should cut it at a 45-degree angle, just below a node (the point where a leaf joins the stem). The cutting should be around 6 inches long and have at least 2-3 healthy leaves. Remove any flowers or buds from the stem, as they can divert energy away from the rooting process.

The next step is to prepare the rooting medium. The ideal medium for rose cuttings is a mixture of peat moss and perlite, as it provides good drainage and aeration for the roots. Alternatively, you can use a mixture of sand and vermiculite or a commercial rooting hormone.

Caring for the cuttings:

Once you have prepared the cutting and rooting medium, it's time to plant the cutting. Make a hole in the rooting medium and insert the cutting, making sure that at least one node is buried below the surface. Firmly press the medium around the cutting to ensure good contact.

Roses are one of the most popular and beautiful flowers, grown for their lovely colors and fragrant blooms. One of the most common ways to propagate roses is through stem cuttings, but these cuttings are prone to fungal infections that can cause significant damage. In this essay, we will discuss how to prevent rose cuttings from fungal infections, with a focus on preventive measures that can be taken before and during the propagation process.

Preventive Measures:

The first step in preventing fungal infections in rose cuttings is to use healthy plants for the cuttings. Plants that are already infected with fungi will transfer the infection to the new cuttings. Therefore, it is important to select plants that are free of any visible signs of fungal infections, such as spots, discolored leaves or stems, or other signs of disease.

Next, it is important to ensure that the cutting tools are clean and sterile. Using dirty or contaminated tools can transfer fungal spores to the cuttings, which can cause infections to spread quickly. To sterilize cutting tools, they can be dipped in rubbing alcohol or a mixture of bleach and water before use.

Another preventive measure is to use a rooting hormone on the cuttings. Rooting hormones contain growth regulators that promote root growth and help the cuttings develop a strong immune system. This will help the cuttings resist fungal infections and other diseases.

Propagation Process:

During the propagation process, it is important to keep the cuttings in a clean and sterile environment. This can be achieved by using sterile soil or rooting medium, and ensuring that the container or pot is clean before planting the cuttings. A layer of sterile sand or perlite can be added to the surface of the soil to prevent fungal spores from settling on the cuttings.

Another important factor in preventing fungal infections is proper watering. Over-watering can lead to fungal growth, so it is important to keep the soil moist but not overly wet. It is also important to avoid getting water on the leaves or stems of the cuttings, as this can create a damp environment that is ideal for fungal growth.

Finally, it is important to monitor the cuttings closely for any signs of fungal infections. Early detection is key to preventing the infection from spreading and causing significant damage. If any signs of infection are detected, such as spots or discoloration on the leaves or stems, it is important to remove the infected cuttings immediately to prevent the infection from spreading to other cuttings.

Preventing fungal infections in rose cuttings requires a combination of preventive measures and proper propagation techniques. By selecting healthy plants, using clean and sterile tools, using rooting hormones, keeping the environment clean and sterile, and monitoring the cuttings closely, gardeners can greatly reduce the risk of fungal infections in their rose cuttings. By following these simple steps, gardeners can enjoy beautiful and healthy roses for years to come.

After planting, the cutting should be kept in a warm, bright, and humid environment. A greenhouse or a plastic bag can be used to create a humid environment around the cutting. It is important to keep the medium moist but not waterlogged, as this can cause the cutting to rot.

Over the next few weeks, the cutting will begin to develop roots. You can check the progress by gently tugging on the cutting; if there is resistance, it means that roots have begun to form. Once the cutting has developed a strong root system, it can be transplanted into a larger container or directly into the ground.

Propagating roses from cuttings can be a rewarding and satisfying experience for any gardener. By following the proper techniques for taking cuttings, preparing the rooting medium, and caring for the cuttings, you can successfully grow healthy and vibrant new roses that are exact clones of the parent plant. While the process may require some patience and attention to detail, the end result is well worth the effort.

CHAPTER 4 PROPAGATION MEDIA

Propagation of roses through root media is a popular method of reproducing roses for gardening and commercial purposes. Root media is used to support and stimulate the growth of roots from the cutting or seedling. Root media consist of different materials with varying physical and chemical properties that affect the growth of roots. This essay will discuss the various root media for rose propagation, their properties, and their suitability for rose propagation.

Types of Root Media for Rose Propagation

There are several types of root media used in rose propagation. These include soil, peat moss, perlite, vermiculite, sand, and various combinations of these materials.

Soil

Soil is a common root medium for rose propagation. Soil is made up of different particles that affect the physical properties of the soil. The particle size of soil can affect the water retention capacity and the porosity of the soil. The pH level of soil is also a critical factor in rose propagation. The ideal pH for rose propagation is between 6.0 and 6.5. If the soil pH is too high or too low, it can affect the absorption of nutrients by the roots.

Peat Moss

Peat moss is another common root medium used in rose propagation. Peat moss is made up of organic material that is decomposed under anaerobic conditions. Peat moss has excellent water retention capacity, making it an ideal root medium for roses. The pH level of peat moss is also important in rose propagation. The ideal pH for peat moss is between 5.5 and 6.0.

Perlite

is a volcanic rock that is heated to high temperatures, causing it to expand. Perlite is lightweight and has excellent drainage properties, making it an ideal root medium for roses. The pH level of perlite is neutral, making it suitable for rose propagation.

Vermiculite

Vermiculite is a mineral that is heated to high temperatures, causing it to expand. Vermiculite is lightweight and has excellent water retention capacity, making it an ideal root medium for roses. The pH level of vermiculite is neutral, making it suitable for rose propagation.

Sand Sand

is a commonly used root medium in rose propagation. Sand has excellent drainage properties, making it ideal for rooting cuttings. The pH level of sand is neutral, making it suitable for rose propagation.

Combinations of Root Media Combining

different types of root media can enhance the physical and chemical properties of the root medium. For example, a combination of soil and perlite can provide good drainage and water retention capacity for rooting cuttings.

Suitability of Root Media for Rose Propagation The suitability of root media for rose propagation depends on several factors, including water retention capacity, drainage properties, pH level, and nutrient content. Roses require a well-draining root medium that retains enough water to keep the roots moist but not waterlogged. The root medium should also have a neutral

pH level,

between 6.0 and 6.5, to allow for optimal nutrient absorption by the roots.

Rose propagation through root media is an important technique for the reproduction of roses for gardening and commercial purposes. Root media consist of different materials with varying physical and chemical properties that affect the growth of roots. Soil, peat moss, perlite, vermiculite, sand, and various combinations of these materials are commonly used as root media for rose propagation. The suitability of root media for rose propagation depends on several factors, including water retention capacity, drainage properties, pH level, and nutrient content. Careful selection of the appropriate root medium is essential for successful rose propagation.

CHAPTER 6 FUNGAL INFECTIONS

One of the biggest challenges when propagating roses through cuttings is preventing fungal infections, which can lead to poor success rates and even death of the cuttings. In this essay, we will discuss different techniques and antifungal treatments to prevent fungal infections in rose cuttings propagation.

Fungal infections in rose cuttings propagation

Fungal infections are one of the biggest challenges when propagating roses through cuttings. Fungi are microscopic organisms that thrive in warm, humid conditions and can be found almost everywhere. Fungal infections can cause a variety of problems, including root rot, stem cankers, and leaf spot, which can weaken the plant and reduce its growth and productivity.

Fungal infections in rose cuttings can be caused by different factors, including poor hygiene practices, contaminated tools, and contaminated growing media. The most common fungal pathogens that affect rose cuttings include Botrytis cinerea, Fusarium oxysporum, and Phytophthora spp. These pathogens can cause a variety of symptoms, including yellowing and wilting of leaves, stunted growth, and root rot.

Preventing fungal infections in rose cuttings propagation

Preventing fungal infections in rose cuttings propagation requires a multi-faceted approach. The following techniques and antifungal treatments can help prevent fungal infections and increase success rates in rose cuttings propagation.

1. **Use healthy plant material**

The first step in preventing fungal infections in rose cuttings propagation is to use healthy plant material. Make sure to select cuttings from healthy, disease-free plants. Avoid using cuttings from plants that show any signs of disease or stress, such as yellowing or wilting leaves. Using healthy plant material will help reduce the risk of introducing fungal pathogens to your cuttings.

2. Maintain good hygiene practices

Maintaining good hygiene practices is essential in preventing fungal infections in rose cuttings propagation. Make sure to clean and sanitize all tools and equipment before use, including pruning shears, scissors, and propagation trays. Use a solution of 70% alcohol or a 10% bleach solution to sanitize tools and equipment. Also, make sure to wash your hands thoroughly before handling cuttings and other plant material.

3. Use a well-draining growing medium

Using a well-draining growing medium is crucial in preventing fungal infections in rose cuttings propagation. A well-draining growing medium will help prevent waterlogging and reduce the risk of root rot. Use a mixture of perlite, vermiculite, and peat moss to create a well-draining growing medium. Also, make sure to sterilize the growing medium before use to kill any potential fungal pathogens.

4. Provide adequate air circulation

Providing adequate air circulation is essential in preventing fungal infections in rose cuttings propagation. Poor air circulation can create a humid environment that promotes fungal growth. Make sure to provide good ventilation and avoid overcrowding your cuttings. Also, make sure to keep your propagation trays clean and free of debris that can trap moisture.

5. Control humidity and temperature

Controlling humidity and temperature is crucial in preventing fungal infections in rose cuttings propagation. Fungal pathogens thrive in warm, humid conditions. Keep your cuttings in a warm, well-lit area, but avoid exposing them to direct sunlight. Also, make sure to monitor the humidity levels and use a humidity dome or misting system to maintain optimal humidity levels.

6. Use anti-fungal treatments

Using antifungal treatments can help prevent fungal infections in rose cuttings propagation. There are different types of antifungal treatments on the market. Use anti-fungal treatments Using anti-fungal treatments can help prevent fungal infections in rose cuttings propagation. There are different types of ant

fungal treatments that can be used, including:

a. Fungicides

Fungicides are chemical compounds that are used to kill or prevent the growth of fungi. There are different types of fungicides available, including contact fungicides and systemic fungicides. Contact fungicides are sprayed on the plant surface and kill the fungi on contact. Systemic fungicides are absorbed by the plant and provide long-lasting protection against fungal infections.

When using fungicides, it is important to follow the manufacturer's instructions carefully. Make sure to use the correct concentration and application method. Also, make sure to apply the fungicide before any fungal infections occur to prevent the spread of the pathogen.

Neem Oil:

Neem oil is a natural product extracted from the seeds of the Neem tree (Azadirachta indica). It contains various compounds, such as azadirachtin, salanin, nimbin, and nimbidin, that have insecticidal, anti-fungal, and antibacterial properties. Neem oil has been used in traditional medicine and agriculture for centuries, and its effectiveness has been supported by scientific studies.

Effectiveness of Neem Oil in Preventing Fungal Diseases in Rose Cutting Propagation:

Several studies have investigated the effectiveness of Neem oil in preventing fungal diseases in various plants, including roses. For instance, a study by El-Mohamedy et al. (2017) found that Neem oil was effective in controlling powdery mildew disease in rose plants. The study used Neem oil at different concentrations (0.25%, 0.5%, and 1%) and compared it to a chemical fungicide (Topas 100EC). The results showed that Neem oil at 1% concentration was as effective as the chemical fungicide in reducing the disease severity and increasing the plant growth.

Similarly, another study by Ali et al. (2018) investigated the efficacy of Neem oil in controlling black spot disease in rose plants. The study used Neem oil at different concentrations (0.25%, 0.5%, and 1%) and compared it to a chemical fungicide (Baycor 25%). The results showed that neem oil at 1% concentration was as effective as the chemical fungicide in reducing the disease severity and increasing the plant growth.

In addition, a study by Singh et al. (2015) evaluated the antifungal activity of Neem oil against various plant pathogenic fungi, including Fusarium oxysporum, which is a common fungal pathogen that affects roses. The study found that neem oil had a significant antifungal effect against all the tested fungi, and its effectiveness was comparable to that of the chemical fungicide (carbendazim).

Moreover, Neem oil has been shown to have other beneficial effects on plant growth and development. For example, a study by Singh et al. (2014) found that Neem oil improved the plant growth and yield of tomato plants and reduced the incidence of various pests and diseases.

Conclusion:

Neem oil is an effective natural product that can prevent fungal diseases in rose cutting propagation. Its anti-fungal and antibacterial properties make it a suitable alternative to chemical fungicides, which can have adverse effects on the environment and human health. Neem oil can be used at different concentrations and in various forms, such as sprays or soil drenches. However, further research is needed to determine the optimal concentration and application method for Neem oil in rose cutting propagation. Nonetheless, the use of Neem oil can provide a safe and sustainable solution to prevent fungal diseases in roses. I highly recommend one of the best Neem products on the market today, it;'s called

AZATEK PLUS

which at this time is only sold at www.CASHYOURGREENS.com

b. Essential oils

Essential oils are natural plant extracts that have anti fungal properties. Some essential oils, such as tea tree oil, clove oil, and eucalyptus oil, have been shown to be effective in preventing fungal infections in plants. To use essential oils, dilute a few drops in water and spray the solution on the plant surface. Essential oils can also be added to the growing medium to prevent fungal infections.

c. Biological controls

Biological controls are living organisms that are used to control the growth of fungal pathogens. Some biological controls, such as Trichoderma spp. and B   acillus subtilis, have been shown to be effective in preventing fungal infections in plants. These organisms work by competing with the fungal pathogens for nutrients and space, and by producing enzymes and metabolites that are toxic to the fungi.

To use biological controls, apply the organism to the growing medium or spray it on the plant surface. Make sure to follow the manufacturer's instructions carefully.

Preventing fungal infections in rose cuttings propagation requires a multi-faceted approach that includes using healthy plant material, maintaining good hygiene practices, using a well-draining growing medium, providing adequate air circulation, controlling humidity and temperature, and using antifungal treatments. By following these techniques and treatments, you can increase the success rate of your rose cuttings propagation and produce healthy, disease-free plants. However, it is important to note that prevention is always better than cure. Therefore, it is important to take preventive measures to minimize the risk of fungal infections in your rose cuttings.

CHAPTER 7 ROOTING HORMONES

Rooting hormones are essential plant growth regulators that can stimulate the growth of roots in plant cuttings. These hormones are vital to the propagation of plants through cuttings, a common method used in horticulture to produce new plants. This essay aims to explore the nature of rooting hormones, their types, their functions, and their applications in plant propagation.

Rooting hormones, also known as auxins, are naturally occurring plant hormones responsible for the initiation and growth of new roots in plants. Auxins are synthesized in the plant's apical meristem, or the growing tip, and are transported throughout the plant via the phloem and xylem. In rooting hormones, auxins are typically found in high concentrations, making them a potent stimulant for root growth.

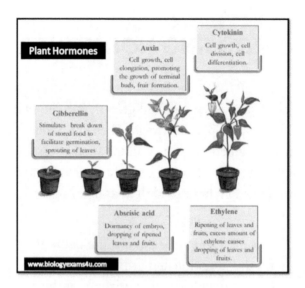

The primary function of rooting hormones is to promote the growth of new roots in plant cuttings. Plant cuttings are parts of a plant that are removed from the parent plant and placed in a growing medium to develop new roots and eventually grow into a new plant. Rooting hormones work by stimulating the cells in the cutting to produce new roots. They promote cell division, elongation, and differentiation, leading to the formation of a healthy root system.

Rooting hormones come in various types, including synthetic and natural hormones. Synthetic hormones are chemically synthesized compounds designed to mimic the effects of natural hormones. These hormones are often more potent and longer-lasting than natural hormones. Natural hormones, on the other hand, are derived from plant extracts or other organic materials. They are less potent and shorter-lasting than synthetic hormones but are generally considered safer and more environmentally friendly.

One of the most commonly used synthetic rooting hormones is indole-3-butyric acid (IBA). IBA is a potent hormone that stimulates root growth in a wide range of plant species. It is available in various forms, including powders, liquids, and gels. Another commonly used synthetic hormone is naphthalene acetic acid (NAA). NAA is less potent than IBA but is still effective in promoting root growth in a wide range of plants.

Natural rooting hormones include substances such as willow bark, honey, and cinnamon. Willow bark contains salicylic acid, which can stimulate root growth in cuttings. Honey contains natural enzymes that promote cell division and root development. Cinnamon contains a substance called cinnamic acid, which can stimulate the growth of new roots.

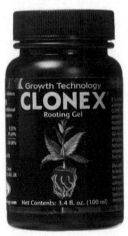

The use of rooting hormones in plant propagation is essential for several reasons. Firstly, rooting hormones can significantly increase the success rate of plant propagation from cuttings. Without rooting hormones, many cuttings would fail to develop roots and eventually die. Secondly, rooting hormones can significantly reduce the time required for plants to establish themselves. Cuttings treated with rooting hormones can develop roots faster, allowing them to establish themselves in a growing medium more quickly. Finally, rooting hormones can enable the propagation of rare or difficult-to-grow plants. By promoting the growth of new roots in cuttings, rooting hormones can allow horticulturists to propagate plants that would otherwise be difficult to grow from seeds or other methods.

Rooting hormones are essential plant growth regulators that can stimulate the growth of roots in plant cuttings. These hormones are vital to the propagation of plants through cuttings, a common method used in horticulture to produce new plants. Rooting hormones come in various types, including synthetic and natural hormones. Synthetic hormones are chemically synthesized compounds designed to mimic the effects of natural hormones, while natural hormones are derived from plant extracts or other organic materials. The use of rooting hormones in plant propagation is essential for increasing the success rate of plant propagation from cuttings, reducing the time required for plants to establish themselves, and enabling the propagation of rare or difficult-to-grow plants.

Now let's take a closer look at some of these rooting hormones and see which one is the best for rooting rose cuttings.

WILLOW TREE CUTTINGS

Effectiveness:

Willow tree cuttings have been found to contain natural hormones called auxin's, which stimulate root growth in plants. The most common auxin found in willow trees is indole-3-butyric acid (IBA), which is also found in many synthetic rooting hormones. Studies have shown that willow tree cuttings can be just as effective as synthetic rooting hormones in promoting root growth in plants (Hartmann et al., 2011).

One study conducted by Lofthouse and Begg (2001) found that willow tree cuttings were effective in promoting root growth in a variety of plant species, including apple, pear, and blackcurrant. The researchers found that cuttings taken from willow trees in the spring were the most effective in promoting root growth, as they contained the highest levels of auxins. Cuttings taken from younger trees were also found to be more effective than those taken from older trees, as younger trees contained higher levels of auxins.

Method of Application:

To use willow tree cuttings as a rooting hormone, gardeners and farmers must first prepare a solution using the cuttings. The first step is to collect several willow tree branches and remove the leaves, twigs, and small branches. The remaining branches are then cut into small pieces, about 1-2 inches in length.

Next, the willow pieces are placed in a container, such as a mason jar, and covered with water. The container is then left to sit for several days, allowing the water to extract the natural hormones from the willow pieces. After several days, the water should have a brownish tint and a strong smell, indicating that the hormones have been extracted.

To use the solution, gardeners and farmers can either dip the cuttings into the solution or spray the solution onto the plants they wish to propagate. The cuttings should then be planted in a soil mixture that is well-drained and moist.

Benefits:

There are several benefits to using willow tree cuttings as a rooting hormone. First, willow tree cuttings are a natural and sustainable alternative to synthetic rooting hormones. This is important for gardeners and farmers who are looking for ways to reduce their environmental impact.

Second, willow tree cuttings are cost-effective. Unlike synthetic rooting hormones, which can be expensive, willow tree cuttings can be collected for free from local trees.

Finally, willow tree cuttings have been found to promote healthier root growth in plants. This is because the natural hormones in willow trees are more balanced than those found in synthetic rooting hormones, which can lead to over stimulation of root growth and decreased plant health.

Willow tree cuttings are an effective and natural alternative to synthetic rooting hormones. They contain natural auxins that stimulate root growth in plants and can be just as effective as synthetic rooting hormones. Willow tree cuttings are also cost-effective and sustainable, making them a popular choice for gardeners and farmers who are looking for ways to reduce their environmental impact. By using willow tree cuttings as a rooting hormone, gardeners and farmers can promote healthier root growth in plants and produce more plants without the need for expensive seeds or plants.

CINNAMON

Plant propagation is a critical aspect of horticulture that is necessary for the production of high-quality plant materials. Rooting is an essential process in plant propagation that allows for the development of new roots from cuttings or other plant parts. The use of rooting hormones or agents is a common practice in horticulture to enhance root growth and development. Cinnamon is a popular natural rooting agent that has gained significant attention in recent years due to its potential efficacy and safety. This essay aims to examine the effectiveness of cinnamon as a rooting agent for plants and explore the scientific evidence supporting its use.

Background

Cinnamon is a spice derived from the inner bark of trees from the genus Cinnamomum. It has been widely used in traditional medicine for its various health benefits, including its anti-inflammatory, antimicrobial, and antioxidant properties. In recent years, cinnamon has gained attention in horticulture as a potential natural rooting agent. The primary active ingredient in cinnamon is cinnamaldehyde, a chemical compound that has been shown to promote root growth and development in plants.

Rooting agents, also known as rooting hormones, are substances used to stimulate the growth of roots from cuttings or other plant parts. These hormones work by triggering the cells in the plant's tissue to divide and differentiate into

56

root cells. Synthetic rooting hormones such as indole-3-butyric acid (IBA) and naphthaleneacetic acid (NAA) are commonly used in commercial horticulture. However, natural alternatives such as cinnamon are becoming increasingly popular due to their safety, affordability, and sustainability.

Effectiveness of Cinnamon as a Rooting Agent

Several studies have investigated the efficacy of cinnamon as a rooting agent for various plant species. In a study by Blythe and Sibley (2014), cinnamon was compared to IBA and NAA in promoting the rooting of stem cuttings from rosemary (Rosmarinus officinalis) and lavender (Lavandula angustifolia). The results showed that cinnamon was as effective as IBA and NAA in promoting rooting, with a rooting percentage of 80% for all treatments.

Another study by Shrestha et al. (2017) evaluated the effectiveness of cinnamon as a rooting agent for cutting propagation of fig (Ficus carica). The study found that cinnamon significantly improved rooting percentage, root length, and root biomass compared to the control treatment. The authors suggested that cinnamon could be used as an alternative to synthetic rooting hormones in fig propagation.

In a study by Ali and Abul-Soad (2020), the effect of cinnamon on the rooting of olive (Olea europaea) cuttings was investigated. The study found that cinnamon significantly increased rooting percentage, root length, and root biomass compared to the control treatment. The authors concluded that cinnamon could be used as a safe and effective alternative to synthetic rooting hormones in olive propagation.

These studies suggest that cinnamon is an effective rooting agent for a variety of plant species. Cinnamon has been shown to improve rooting percentage, root length, and root biomass, which are important indicators of root growth and development.

Mechanism of Action

The mechanism by which cinnamon promotes root growth and development is not fully understood. However, it is believed to involve the cinnamaldehyde compound, which has been shown to stimulate the activity of enzymes involved in cell division and differentiation. Cinnamaldehyde has also been shown to increase the levels of auxins, a class of plant hormones that play a critical role in root development.

Cinnamaldehyde may also act as an antimicrobial agent, protecting the cuttings from fungal and bacterial infections that can inhibit rooting. This property is particularly useful in organic horticulture, where the use of synthetic fungicides and bactericides is restricted.

Cinnamaldehyde may also act as an antimicrobial agent, protecting the cuttings from fungal and bacterial infections that can inhibit rooting. This property is particularly useful in organic horticulture, where the use of synthetic fungicides and bactericides is restricted.

There are two main types of cinnamon: Ceylon cinnamon (also known as "true cinnamon") and cassia cinnamon. Ceylon cinnamon is a more expensive and less common variety, while cassia cinnamon is more widely available and less expensive.

Some gardeners and DIY enthusiasts recommend using Ceylon cinnamon because it contains less coumarin, a compound that can be toxic in large amounts. However, the amount of coumarin present in the small amount of cinnamon used for rooting agents is unlikely to be harmful to plants.

Ultimately, the choice of which type of cinnamon to use as a rooting agent is up to personal preference. Both Ceylon cinnamon and cassia cinnamon have been used successfully as rooting agents, so it is more important to ensure that the cinnamon is fresh and of high quality.

In conclusion, cinnamon has shown promise as a natural rooting agent for plants. Studies have demonstrated its efficacy in promoting root growth and development in various plant species. Cinnamaldehyde, the primary active ingredient in cinnamon, is believed to stimulate cell division and differentiation, increase auxin levels, and act as an antimicrobial agent. These properties make cinnamon a safe, affordable, and sustainable alternative to synthetic rooting hormones. While further research is needed to fully understand the mechanism of action of cinnamon, the evidence so far suggests that it can be a valuable tool in horticulture for improving plant propagation success. Horticulturists and growers can consider using cinnamon as a natural and effective rooting agent for their plants.

HONEY

Rooting is an essential process in the growth and development of plants. It involves the growth of roots from the cutting or stem of a plant, which can then be transplanted to a new location. The process of rooting can be challenging, and many gardeners and plant growers turn to rooting agents to improve the success of the process. One such agent is honey, which has been used as a rooting agent for many years. This essay will explore the effectiveness of honey as a rooting agent for plants.

What is Honey?

Honey is a natural sweet substance produced by bees from the nectar of flowers. The nectar is collected by bees and then converted into honey through a process of regurgitation and evaporation. Honey is a complex mixture of sugars, vitamins, minerals, and other components, including enzymes and amino acids.

Honey as a Rooting Agent:

Honey has been used as a rooting agent for many years, and its effectiveness has been the subject of several studies. Honey contains natural plant growth hormones, which can help stimulate root growth in plants. Additionally, honey has antimicrobial and antifungal properties, which can help prevent infections in the cutting or stem of a plant during the rooting process.

Studies have shown that honey can be effective in promoting root growth in a variety of plants. For example, a study published in the journal Plant Physiology and Biochemistry" found that honey was effective in promoting root growth in basil and oregano plants. The study compared the rooting performance of these plants using honey, IBA (a synthetic rooting hormone), and water as a control. The results showed that honey was just as effective as IBA in promoting root growth, and both were significantly better than water.

Another study published in the journal "Scientia Horticulturae" found that honey was effective in promoting root growth in rosemary plants. The study compared the rooting performance of rosemary plants using honey, IBA, and water as a control. The results showed that honey was as effective as IBA in promoting root growth, and both were significantly better than water.

Benefits of Using Honey as a Rooting Agent:

One of the main benefits of using honey as a rooting agent is that it is a natural and environmentally friendly option. Synthetic rooting hormones can be expensive and may contain chemicals that can be harmful to the environment. Honey, on the other hand, is a natural substance that does not have any harmful environmental effects.

Another benefit of using honey as a rooting agent is that it has antimicrobial and antifungal properties, which can help prevent infections in the cutting or stem of a plant during the rooting process. This can be especially important when rooting plants in soil or other planting mediums that may contain harmful bacteria or fungi.

Additionally, honey is readily available and easy to use. It can be applied directly to the cutting or stem of a plant without the need for complicated mixing or preparation.

Drawbacks of Using Honey as a Rooting Agent:

While honey can be an effective rooting agent, there are some drawbacks to using it. One of the main drawbacks is that honey can be sticky and may attract insects or other pests to the plant. This can be especially problematic when rooting plants indoors or in areas with high insect activity.

Additionally, honey may not be as effective as synthetic rooting hormones in promoting root growth in some plant species. While studies have shown that honey can be effective in promoting root growth in many plants, there may be some plant species that do not respond as well to honey as they do to synthetic rooting hormones.

In conclusion, honey can be an effective rooting agent for many plant species. It contains natural plant growth hormones and has antimicrobial and antifungal properties, which can help promote root growth and prevent infections during the rooting process. Additionally, honey is a natural and environmentally friendly option that is readily available and easy to use. However, it is important to consider the potential drawbacks of using honey as a rooting agent, such as its sticky consistency and the possibility that it may attract insects or other pests to the plant. Moreover, while honey has been shown to be effective in promoting root growth in many plant species, it may not be as effective as synthetic rooting hormones in some cases.

Overall, the effectiveness of honey as a rooting agent for plants makes it a valuable option for gardeners and plant growers. Its natural properties and ease of use make it an attractive alternative to synthetic rooting hormones, particularly for those who are environmentally conscious or prefer natural options. However, it is essential to consider the specific plant species and environmental factors when deciding whether to use honey as a rooting agent or to opt for synthetic hormones. Further research could help determine the specific conditions under which honey is most effective and how it can be best utilized in the rooting process.

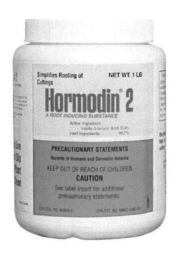

CHAPTER 9 WERE WE SUCCESSFUL?

Rose cutting propagation is a popular technique for growing new rose plants. It is a cost-effective and reliable way to produce new plants that are genetically identical to the parent plant. However, not all rose cuttings will successfully root and grow into new plants. It is important to know the signs of successful rose cutting propagation to ensure that the cutting has rooted and is growing healthily. In this essay, we will discuss the various signs that indicate a successful rose cutting propagation.

Appearance of New Growth

The appearance of new growth is one of the most obvious signs of successful rose cutting propagation. Once the cutting has been planted, it will take a few weeks or months for new growth to appear. The new growth will typically be seen as small green shoots emerging from the base of the cutting or from the node where the leaves were removed. These shoots are a sign that the cutting has successfully rooted and is starting to grow.

It is important to note that the appearance of new growth is not always a guarantee of successful propagation. Sometimes, rose cuttings may produce new growth but fail to develop roots. This is known as top growth or leafy cuttings, where the cutting may continue to produce new shoots but eventually wither and die. Therefore, it is essential to inspect the cutting for other signs of successful propagation.

Healthy Leaves and Stems

Another sign of successful rose cutting propagation is the presence of healthy leaves and stems. When a cutting successfully roots and starts to grow, it should have a healthy appearance. The leaves should be green and turgid, indicating that the plant is receiving the necessary nutrients and water. The stem should be firm and upright, supporting the plant and allowing it to grow.

If the leaves and stems are unhealthy or wilted, it may be a sign that the cutting has not rooted properly or that the plant is not receiving adequate nutrients and water. Leaves that are discolored, yellowed, or brown may indicate nutrient deficiencies or fungal infections. Similarly, wilted or drooping stems may indicate root rot or insufficient water uptake. It is important to address these issues promptly to ensure the survival of the cutting.

Root Development

Root development is a critical aspect of successful rose cutting propagation. When a cutting is planted, it must develop a robust root system to anchor itself in the soil and absorb water and nutrients. If the cutting has successfully rooted, it should have a healthy root system. This can be checked by gently lifting the cutting from the soil and inspecting the roots.

Healthy roots should be white or light brown in color, firm and fleshy, and should extend outwards from the stem. If there are no roots visible or the roots are brown, mushy, or discolored, it indicates that the cutting has not successfully rooted. The root system of a cutting may take a few weeks or months to develop fully, depending on the plant species and environmental conditions.

Resistance to Tugging

When a rose cutting has successfully rooted, it will have a good grip on the soil and will resist tugging. This is because the roots have grown and anchored themselves into the soil. To test for resistance, gently tug on the stem of the cutting. If the stem resists your tug, it is a sign that the cutting has successfully rooted and is growing healthily.

Conversely, if the stem easily comes out of the soil, it may be a sign that the cutting has not rooted properly or that the root system is weak. In such cases, it may be necessary to replant the cutting or provide additional support until the root system has fully developed.

No Signs of Disease or Pests

A successful rose cutting propagation will show no signs of disease or pests. If the cutting is infected with a disease or has pest damage, it may not grow or may die soon after

No Signs of Disease or Pests

A successful rose cutting propagation will show no signs of disease or pests. If the cutting is infected with a disease or has pest damage, it may not grow or may die soon after rooting. It is important to inspect the cutting regularly for any signs of disease or pest damage. Common signs of disease include wilting, discoloration of leaves or stems, and the presence of fungal growth. Pest damage may be visible as holes or bite marks on the leaves or stems, or the presence of insects such as Aphids, Spider mites, or Thrips.

Prevention of disease and pest damage is crucial in ensuring the success of rose cutting propagation. This can be achieved through good plant hygiene practices, such as sterilizing cutting tools and pots before use, and regularly cleaning and disinfecting the planting area. In addition, monitoring t

he cutting for any signs of disease or pests and promptly addressing any issues that arise can help prevent further damage.

In conclusion, there are several signs that indicate a successful rose cutting propagation. These include the appearance of new growth, healthy leaves and stems, root development, resistance to tugging, and no signs of disease or pests. It is important to monitor the cutting regularly for these signs and to address any issues promptly to ensure the success of the propagation.

Successful rose cutting propagation requires patience, attention to detail and proper care. It is important to provide the cutting with the necessary nutrients, water, and sunlight to promote healthy growth. In addition, providing adequate support and protection from external factors such as wind or extreme temperatures can help the cutting thrive.

Overall, rose cutting propagation is a rewarding and cost-effective way to grow new rose plants. With proper care and attention, a successful propagation can result in a beautiful and healthy rose plant that will provide joy for years to come.

CHAPTER 9   AIR LAYERING ROSES PROCEDURE

Propagation of roses is an important aspect in horticulture as it allows for the production of new plants from existing ones. Air layering is one of the propagation methods that has gained popularity among rose growers due to its ease and efficiency in producing healthy and well-rooted plants. This essay will discuss the air layering technique and its application in propagating roses. The essay will cover the history and background of air layering, the benefits and drawbacks of air layering, the process of air layering roses, and its success rate.

Background

Air layering is a propagation technique that dates back to ancient China and Japan, where it was used to propagate fruit trees. It involves creating a new plant from an existing one by inducing roots to grow on a stem without removing it from the mother plant. This is done by making a small cut or wound on the stem, and then wrapping it with moist sphagnum moss or peat moss and a protective layer of plastic. The wound triggers the plant's natural response to produce roots, and the moist medium provides the necessary moisture and nutrients for root development.

Benefits and Drawbacks Air layering

has numerous benefits that make it an attractive propagation method for rose growers. Firstly, it allows for the production of new plants that are identical to the parent plant in terms of genetic makeup and characteristics. This is especially important for rose cultivars that have desirable traits such as flower color, fragrance, and disease resistance, as growers can produce more of these plants without relying on seeds that may not produce plants with the same traits. Secondly, air layering allows for the production of mature plants that are ready to be transplanted once they have rooted. This means that growers can produce plants that are ready for sale or planting in a shorter time compared to other propagation methods such as seed sowing or cutting. Thirdly, air layering is a simple and low-cost propagation method that can be done with minimal equipment and materials.

However, air layering also has some drawbacks that growers should consider before using it as a propagation method. Firstly, it is not suitable for all plant species, as some plants may not respond well to the technique. Secondly, it requires more time and effort compared to other propagation methods such as cutting or seed sowing, as the process of inducing root growth can take several weeks or even months. Finally, air layering can also be affected by environmental factors such as temperature and humidity, which can affect the success rate of the technique.

Process of Air Layering Roses The process of air layering roses involves the following steps:

1. Selecting the stem: Choose a healthy, young stem that is at least pencil-thick in diameter and has no signs of damage or disease. The stem should also have at least one node where leaves or buds are attached.

2. Making a cut: Make a small cut or wound in the stem about 1 inch long, using a sharp knife or blade. The cut should be deep enough to expose the inner bark but not deep enough to cut through the entire stem.

3. Applying rooting hormone: Apply rooting hormone to the cut area to stimulate root growth. Rooting hormone can be purchased from garden centers or online stores.

4. Wrapping the stem: Wrap the cut area with moist sphagnum moss or peat moss, making sure to cover the entire cut area. Then, cover the moss with a plastic bag or wrap to keep it moist and secure.

5. Securing the wrap: Tie the plastic wrap or bag securely around the moss-covered stem using a string or wire. Make sure that the wrap is tight enough to hold the moss in place but not so tight that it cuts off the circulation to the stem.

6. Monitoring the plant: Check the moss and plastic wrap regularly to make

Monitoring the plant: Check the moss and plastic wrap regularly to make

sure that they are still moist and in place. If the moss becomes dry, spray it with water to keep it moist. If the plastic wrap or bag becomes loose, retie it securely.

7. Root development: After several weeks or months, roots should start to develop on the stem, just below the cut area. Once the roots are about 1-2 inches long, the air layer can be removed from the mother plant.

8. Planting: Carefully remove the plastic wrap and moss from the rooted stem, being careful not to damage the roots. Plant the new rose plant in a pot or directly in the ground, making sure that the soil is well-draining and that the plant receives adequate sunlight and water.

Success Rate The success rate of air layering roses varies depending on the cultivar, environmental conditions, and the skill of the grower. However, with proper technique and care, air layering can have a high success rate of up to 90%.

One of the factors that can affect the success rate of air layering is the timing of the process. Air layering is best done during the active growth period of the plant, usually in spring or early summer when the plant is producing new growth. This is because the plant's natural response to wound healing and root growth is more active during this period.

Another factor that can affect the success rate is the condition of the stem and the wound area. The stem should be healthy and free from damage or disease, and the wound should be clean and free from any debris that may inhibit root growth. The use of rooting hormone can also help to stimulate root growth and increase the success rate of the technique.

Finally, environmental factors such as temperature and humidity can also affect the success rate of air layering. The ideal temperature for air layering is between 70-80°F (21-27°C), and the humidity should be high enough to keep the moss moist but not too high that it causes rot or mold to develop.

Conclusion

In conclusion, air layering is a useful and effective propagation technique that can be used to produce new rose plants that are identical to the parent plant in terms of genetic makeup and characteristics. It is a simple and low-cost method that can be done with minimal equipment and materials, and it produces mature plants that are ready for transplanting in a shorter time compared to other propagation methods. However, the success rate of air layering can be affected by various factors, including environmental conditions, the condition of the stem, and the skill of the grower. Therefore, growers should follow proper technique and care to increase the success rate of air layering and produce healthy and well-rooted rose plants.

CHAPTER 10 POTTING IT UP

If you have recently acquired a rooting rose cutting and are wondering how to transplant it into a pot without harming it, this essay will provide you with a step-by-step guide to ensure your rose cutting survives the transplantation process.

Step 1: Choose the right pot

When transplanting a rooting rose cutting into a pot, it is essential to choose the right pot size. A pot that is too small will restrict the growth of the roots, while a pot that is too big will result in waterlogging and root rot. Ideally, you should choose a pot that is one size larger than the current pot. This will allow the roots to expand and grow, and the plant to thrive.

Step 2: Prepare the potting mix

The potting mix is critical for the success of the rose cutting transplantation. You should choose a high-quality potting mix that is well-draining and nutrient-rich. A mix of peat moss, perlite, and vermiculite is ideal. Avoid using garden soil as it may contain pathogens that can harm the plant.

Step 3: Water the rose cutting

Before transplanting the rose cutting, it is essential to water it thoroughly. This will ensure that the roots are hydrated and prevent them from drying out during the transplantation process.

Step 4: Gently remove the rose cutting from the current pot

To remove the rose cutting from the current pot, gently tap the sides of the pot and loosen the soil around the plant. Carefully lift the plant out of the pot, holding it by the stem and avoiding touching the roots.

Step 5: Loosen the roots

Once the plant is out of the pot, use your fingers to loosen the roots gently. This will help the roots to spread out in the new pot and take hold of the potting mix.

Step 6: Add the potting mix to the new pot

Fill the new pot with potting mix, leaving enough space for the rose cutting to sit comfortably. Make a hole in the center of the potting mix for the rose cutting.

Step 7: Plant the rose cutting

Place the rose cutting in the hole, ensuring that the roots are covered with potting mix. The top of the root ball should be level with the surface of the potting mix.

Step 8: Water the rose cutting

After planting the rose cutting, water it thoroughly to settle the potting mix and remove any air pockets around the roots. Continue to water the plant regularly, ensuring that the potting mix remains moist but not waterlogged.

Step 9: Place the pot in a suitable location

The location of the pot is critical for the success of the rose cutting transplantation. Choose a location that receives adequate sunlight and has good air circulation. Avoid placing the pot in areas that are prone to strong winds, as this can damage the plant.

Step 10: Provide support for the rose cutting

If the rose cutting is tall or has thin stems, you may need to provide support for it. Use a stake or bamboo pole and tie the plant to it using soft twine. This will prevent the plant from bending or breaking due to wind or rain.

Transplanting a rooting rose cutting into a pot can be a delicate process that requires care and attention. By following the above steps, you can ensure that your rose cutting survives the transplantation process and thrives in its new home. Remember to choose the right pot size, prepare the potting mix, water the plant, gently remove the rose cutting from the current pot, loosen the roots, add the potting mix to the new pot, plant the rose cutting, water the plant, place the pot in a suitable location, and provide support if necessary.

However, it is important to note that the success of the transplantation process also depends on external factors such as temperature, humidity, and pests. To ensure that your rose cutting continues to thrive, you should monitor its growth and health regularly and take appropriate measures to address any issues that arise.

In addition to the transplantation process, there are other factors that can influence the growth and health of your rose plant, such as pruning, fertilizing, and disease control. Learning about these aspects of rose care can help you create an optimal environment for your plant to grow and flourish.

Pruning is an essential part of rose care, as it helps to maintain the shape and size of the plant, remove dead or damaged branches, and promote healthy growth. Pruning should be done during the dormant season, typically in late winter or early spring, before the plant begins to actively grow. When pruning, it is important to use sharp and clean pruning shears to prevent damage to the plant.

Fertilizing is another critical aspect of rose care, as it provides the necessary nutrients for the plant to grow and bloom. Roses require a balanced fertilizer that contains nitrogen, phosphorus, and potassium, as well as trace elements such as iron and magnesium. Fertilizer should be applied during the growing season, typically every 4-6 weeks, following the manufacturer's instructions.

Disease control is also important for rose care, as roses are susceptible to various fungal diseases such as black spot and powdery mildew. To prevent and control these diseases, you should maintain good hygiene practices such as removing dead leaves and debris, providing adequate air circulation, and avoiding overhead watering. If disease symptoms appear, you should take appropriate measures such as applying fungicides or removing affected plant parts.

In conclusion, transplanting a rooting rose cutting into a pot requires careful attention and adherence to specific steps. By following the recommended steps, you can provide the optimal conditions for your rose cutting to thrive in its new pot. However, it is important to note that rose care is an ongoing process that involves regular monitoring and maintenance. By learning about the various aspects of rose care such as pruning, fertilizing, and disease control, you can create an ideal environment for your rose plant to grow and flourish.

CHAPTER 11 ROSE DISEASES

Introduction

Roses are one of the most popular flowering plants in the world, prized for their beauty, fragrance, and versatility. However, like all plants, they are susceptible to a range of diseases that can impact their health and growth. In this essay, we will examine the top five diseases that affect roses, including their causes, symptoms, and treatment options.

Black Spot

Black spot is a significant fungal disease that affects roses, causing severe defoliation and weakening the plant. It is caused by the fungus Diplocarpon rosae, and it is one of the most common diseases of rose plants worldwide. This essay aims to explore the different aspects of black spot disease in roses, including its symptoms, causes, and control measures. Additionally, it will analyze the impact of this disease on the commercial production of roses and the steps that can be taken to prevent and manage the disease.

Symptoms of Black Spot Disease in Roses

Black spot is characterized by the development of black or brown spots on the leaves of rose plants. The spots are circular, and they usually start small

and grow to about 1/2 inch in diameter. As the disease progresses, the spots merge, and the affected leaves turn yellow and eventually fall off. In severe cases, the disease can defoliate the entire plant, leading to its eventual death.

Apart from the spots and defoliation, other symptoms of black spot include leaf curling, stunted growth, and premature flower drop. Infected leaves also have a characteristic fringed appearance, which is caused by the fungal spores that grow on the leaf margins. Additionally, the disease can cause stem cankers and weaken the plant's overall vigor, making it more susceptible to other diseases and pests.

Causes of Black Spot Disease in Roses

Black spot is caused by the fungus Diplocarpon rosae, which thrives in warm and humid conditions. The spores of the fungus can survive on fallen leaves and other plant debris for up to two years, making it challenging to control the disease once it has established itself in a garden or commercial rose farm. Additionally, the fungus can spread rapidly through water splashes, wind, and infected pruning tools.

The disease is more prevalent in areas with high humidity and rainfall, and it tends to affect older leaves first before spreading to younger leaves. This is because older leaves are less able to defend themselves against the disease and have weaker cell walls that are easier to penetrate by the fungal spores.

Control Measures for Black Spot Disease in Roses

The control of black spot disease in roses involves a combination of cultural, chemical, and biological measures. Cultural control measures include maintaining good hygiene in the garden or commercial farm by removing fallen leaves and other plant debris. This prevents the buildup of fungal spores and reduces the risk of infection. Additionally, it is essential to water the plants in the morning to allow the leaves to dry out during the day, reducing the humidity levels that favor the growth of the fungus.

Another cultural control measure is to plant disease-resistant rose varieties. These roses are bred to be resistant to black spot and other fungal diseases and can reduce the risk of infection. It is also essential to provide adequate spacing between rose plants to promote air circulation, which can help reduce humidity levels and prevent the spread of the disease.

Chemical control measures

involve the use of fungicides to control the disease. These fungicides are applied as a spray to the foliage and can effectively kill the fungus or prevent its growth. However, the use of fungicides should be limited to when other control measures have failed, as over-reliance on fungicides can lead to the development of fungicide-resistant strains of the fungus.

Biological control

measures involve the use of beneficial microorganisms and insects to control the disease. These include the use of compost tea and other microbial inoculants that promote soil health and increase the plant's ability to resist the disease. Additionally, predatory insects such as ladybugs and lacewings can be used to control the population of insects that spread the disease, such as aphids.

Impact of Black Spot Disease on the Commercial Production of Roses

Impact of Black Spot Disease on the Commercial Production of Roses Black spot disease can have a significant impact on the commercial production of roses, especially in regions where rose cultivation is a major economic activity. The disease can cause significant yield losses and reduce the quality of the roses produced, leading to lower prices and reduced profitability.

One of the main impacts of black spot disease on commercial rose production is reduced yield. Infected plants produce fewer flowers, and the flowers themselves may be smaller and of lower quality. This can lead to reduced profits for commercial rose growers, as they are unable to produce the same quantity and quality of roses that they would be able to if their plants were not infected with black spot disease.

Additionally, black spot disease can reduce the lifespan of rose plants, leading to the need for more frequent replanting. This can be a significant cost for commercial growers, as replanting requires the purchase of new plants, labor to remove the old plants, and preparation of the soil for new plants. Replanting also leads to a loss of production during the time it takes for the new plants to mature and begin producing flowers.

The impact of black spot disease on commercial rose production is not limited to direct yield losses and replanting costs. The disease can also lead to higher labor costs and increased use of chemical controls, as growers may need to spend more time and money controlling the disease to prevent its spread. This can further reduce profits for growers, especially small-scale growers who may not have the resources to invest in expensive control measures.

In addition to economic impacts, black spot disease can also have environmental impacts. The use of chemical controls to manage the disease can lead to increased chemical runoff and pollution, which can harm local ecosystems and wildlife. This can have long-term impacts on the health of the environment and the sustainability of rose cultivation in the region.

Prevention and Management of Black Spot Disease in Roses

Preventing and managing black spot disease in roses requires a combination of cultural, chemical, and biological control measures. One of the most effective control measures is maintaining good garden hygiene, which involves removing fallen leaves and other plant debris regularly. This reduces the amount of fungal spores in the environment and reduces the risk of infection.

Another effective control measure is planting disease-resistant rose varieties. Many commercial rose cultivars are bred to be resistant to black spot disease, and growers can choose to plant these varieties to reduce the risk of infection. Additionally, providing adequate spacing between plants and promoting good air circulation can help reduce humidity levels and prevent the spread of the disease.

Chemical control measures should be used as a last resort and only when other control measures have failed. Fungicides can be effective in controlling the disease, but their use should be limited to prevent the development of fungicide-resistant strains of the fungus. Additionally, growers should follow label instructions carefully when using fungicides and use them only in recommended amounts and at recommended times.

Biological control measures can also be effective in managing black spot disease. The use of beneficial microorganisms and insects can promote soil health and increase the plant's ability to resist the disease. Additionally, predatory insects can be used to control the population of insects that spread the disease.

Black spot disease is a significant fungal disease that affects roses, causing severe defoliation and weakening the plant. It is caused by the fungus Diplocarpon rosae and is one of the most common diseases of rose plants worldwide. The disease can have a significant impact on the commercial production of roses, leading to reduced yield, quality, and profitability. Prevention and management of the disease require a combination of cultural, chemical, and biological control measures, including good garden hygiene, disease-resistant rose varieties, and limited use of fungicides. By implementing these control measures, growers can reduce the risk of black spot disease and ensure the sustainability of rose cultivation in their region.

Powdery Mildew

Powdery mildew is a fungal disease that is common on roses. This disease affects the leaves and flowers of roses and can cause serious damage if left untreated. Powdery mildew is caused by different fungi, which belong to the Erysiphaceae family. This disease is easily identifiable by the powdery white or gray patches that appear on the leaves and stems of affected plants. The fungus grows on the surface of the plant, and it does not require water to germinate, which makes it easy to spread from plant to plant. This essay will explore the causes, symptoms, and treatment of powdery mildew on roses.

Causes

Powdery mildew is caused by several species of fungi belonging to the Erysiphaceae family. These fungi thrive in warm, humid environments, and they can infect roses at any stage of growth. The fungi spread by producing spores that are carried by the wind or insects from infected plants to healthy ones. The spores can survive for a long time in the soil, and they can be transported over long distances by wind or water.

Several factors can contribute to the development of powdery mildew on roses. These factors include:

1. **Humidity**: Powdery mildew thrives in high humidity environments. If the air around the roses is humid, it creates the perfect environment for the fungi to grow.

2. **Poor air circulation**: Poor air circulation around the roses can also contribute to the development of powdery mildew. If the air is stagnant, the humidity around the roses increases, which creates a perfect environment fo the fungi to grow.

3. **Soil conditions**: The fungi that cause powdery mildew can survive in the soil for a long time. If the soil around the roses is infected, the spores can easily infect the plant.

4. **Temperature:** Powdery mildew thrives in warm temperatures, between 60 and 80 degrees Fahrenheit.

Symptoms

Powdery mildew is easy to identify by the powdery white or gray patches that appear on the leaves and stems of affected plants. These patches are caused by the fungal spores that grow on the surface of the plant. As the disease progresses, the patches can become larger and more extensive, covering the entire plant. In severe cases, the leaves and flowers of the roses can turn yellow and fall off, which can lead to the death of the plant.

Other symptoms of powdery mildew on roses include:

1. Deformed leaves and flowers: The fungal growth can cause the leaves and flowers of the roses to become deformed and stunted.

2. Reduced growth: Powdery mildew can also slow down the growth of the roses, leading to smaller flowers and fewer blooms.

3. Weakened plant: As the disease progresses, it can weaken the plant, making it more susceptible to other diseases and pests.

Treatment

Treating powdery mildew on roses requires a combination of cultural practices and fungicides. The following are some of the methods used to control and treat powdery mildew on roses.

1. **Pruning:** Pruning infected parts of the plant can help control the spread of the disease. Cut off any infected leaves or stems, and dispose of them immediately to prevent the spores from spreading.

2. **Watering**: Water the roses at the base, rather than from above, to reduce humidity around the plant. Also, avoid over-watering, as this can create an environment that is favorable for the growth of the fungi.

3. **Fungicides**: Several fungicides can be used to treat powdery mildew on roses. These fungicides are usually applied as a spray to the leaves and stems of the plant. Some of the commonly used fungicides include sulfur, Neem oil, and potassium bicarbonate. These fungicides work by either killing the spores or preventing them from germinating.

Sulfur is one of the oldest and most effective fungicides for powdery mildew control. It is a contact fungicide that works by inhibiting the growth of the fungus. Sulfur is usually applied as a spray to the leaves and stems of the plant, and it should be applied when the weather is dry and warm.

Neem oil is another effective fungicide for powdery mildew control. It is a natural oil extracted from the seeds of the neem tree, and it works by disrupting the life cycle of the fungus. Neem oil should be applied as a spray to the leaves and stems of the plant, and it should be applied every 7-14 days.

Potassium bicarbonate is a fungicide that works by raising the pH of the plant's surface, making it difficult for the fungus to survive. Potassium bicarbonate is also effective in controlling other fungal diseases, such as black spot and downy mildew. It should be applied as a spray to the leaves and stems of the plant, and it should be applied every 7-14 days.

It is important to follow the instructions on the label when using fungicides to treat powdery mildew on roses. Overuse of fungicides can lead to the development of resistant strains of the fungus, which can be difficult to control.

Prevention

Preventing powdery mildew on roses is easier than treating an established infection. The following are some of the measures that can be taken to prevent powdery mildew on roses:

1. **Plant resistant varieties**: Some rose varieties are resistant to powdery mildew. When planting roses, choose varieties that are resistant to this disease.

2. **Prune regularly:** Pruning regularly can help increase air circulation around the plant, reducing humidity and preventing the development of powdery mildew.

3. **Water correctly**: Water the roses at the base, rather than from above, to reduce humidity around the plant. Also, avoid over-watering, as this can create an environment that is favorable for the growth of the fungi.

4. **Improve soil drainage:** Improving soil drainage around the roses can reduce the chances of powdery mildew developing.

5. **Use fungicides** as a preventative measure: Fungicides can be used as a preventative measure to control the development of powdery mildew. Apply fungicides every 7-14 days, following the instructions on the label.

3. Rust

Rust is a common disease that affects roses. It is caused by a fungal pathogen that can significantly reduce the growth and quality of roses, as well as cause aesthetic damage. Rust is one of the most common rose diseases and can occur in any region where roses are grown. This essay will discuss the causes, symptoms, and management of rust in roses, with a focus on the scientific literature on this topic.

CAUSES OF RUST

Rust is caused by a fungal pathogen known as Phragmidium mucronatum. This pathogen overwinters on infected leaves and can spread to new growth in the spring. The fungal spores are easily spread by wind, water, and even garden tools, which can transport the spores from plant to plant. The fungus prefers warm, humid conditions and can thrive in areas with poor air circulation.

Symptoms of Rust in Roses

The symptoms of rust in roses can be easily identified. The first symptom of rust is the appearance of yellow or orange spots on the upper surface of the leaves. These spots are usually circular or oblong in shape and may be accompanied by small black dots. As the disease progresses, the spots may enlarge and become more numerous. Eventually, the leaves may turn yellow, wilt, and fall off the plant.

Management of Rust in Roses

There are several management strategies that can be employed to control rust in roses. The first and most important step is to remove infected leaves and plant debris from the garden. This will help to prevent the spread of the fungus and reduce the likelihood of reinfection. Additionally, it is important to maintain good garden hygiene by keeping the area around the roses clean and free of debris.

Another important management strategy is to promote good air circulation around the plants. This can be achieved by spacing the plants apart and pruning them regularly to remove dead or diseased wood. It is also important to water the plants in the morning, so that the leaves have time to dry before the evening dew sets in.

Chemical control options are also available for the management of rust in roses. Fungicides containing active ingredients such as propiconazole, myclobutanil, and tebuconazole have been shown to be effective against rust. These fungicides should be applied according to the manufacturer's instructions and may require multiple applications to achieve full control.

Research on Rust in Roses

Several studies have been conducted on the management of rust in roses. In one study, researchers evaluated the efficacy of various fungicides against rust in roses. They found that propiconazole and myclobutanil were the most effective fungicides, providing over 90% control of rust in treated plants. Tebuconazole was also effective, but provided slightly lower levels of control.

Another study evaluated the effect of plant spacing on the incidence of rust in roses. The researchers found that increasing the spacing between plants resulted in lower levels of rust infection. This is likely due to the improved air circulation around the plants, which reduces the likelihood of fungal spores being deposited on the leaves.

A third study evaluated the effectiveness of cultural management practices, such as pruning and removal of infected leaves, on the control of rust in roses. The researchers found that these practices were effective in reducing the incidence and severity of rust in roses.

In conclusion, rust is a common disease that affects roses and can cause significant damage to these plants. The disease is caused by a fungal pathogen that can be easily spread by wind, water, and garden tools. The symptoms of rust are easily identifiable, and include yellow or orange spots on the upper surface of the leaves.

Effective management strategies for rust in roses include removing infected leaves and plant debris, promoting good air circulation around the plants, and using fungicides as necessary. Research has shown that cultural management practices such as pruning and increasing plant spacing can also be effective in controlling rust in roses.

It is important for gardeners to be vigilant and monitor their roses for signs of rust, as early detection and management can prevent the spread of the disease and limit damage to the plants. In addition, implementing good garden hygiene practices, such as cleaning garden tools and equipment, can help to prevent the spread of rust and other fungal diseases.

Overall, the management of rust in roses requires a multifaceted approach that includes both cultural and chemical strategies. By implementing these strategies, gardeners can effectively control rust in their roses and maintain healthy, beautiful plants.

Botrytis Blight

Introduction Botrytis blight, also known as gray mold, is a fungal disease that affects many plants, including roses. The disease is caused by the fungus Botrytis cinerea, which can cause significant damage to roses, leading to a reduction in the quality and quantity of flowers. Botrytis blight is a common problem for rose growers, and it can be challenging to control and prevent. In this essay, we will discuss the symptoms, causes, and management of Botrytis blight in roses.

Symptoms

The symptoms of Botrytis blight in roses can vary depending on the severity of the infection. Initially, small brown spots appear on the petals, leaves, and stem of the rose plant. These spots rapidly enlarge and become

covered with a gray, fuzzy mold. The flowers may wilt and become deformed, and the petals may turn brown and fall off. If left untreated, the disease can spread throughout the plant and eventually kill it.

Causes Botrytis cinerea is a saprophytic fungus that thrives in cool and moist conditions. The fungus overwinters on plant debris, such as dead leaves and stems, and can infect the new growth in the spring. The disease can also spread from plant to plant through spores that are carried by the wind or rain. Roses that are grown in areas with high humidity or that are overcrowded are more susceptible to Botrytis blight.

Management

The management of Botrytis blight in roses involves a combination of cultural practices, chemical treatments, and biological controls. Cultural practices include pruning and removing infected plant debris to reduce the spread of the disease. Good sanitation practices, such as cleaning tools and equipment after use, can also help prevent the disease from spreading.

Chemical treatments,

such as fungicides, can be effective in controlling Botrytis blight. However, they should be used judiciously and only when necessary. Overuse of fungicides can lead to the development of resistance in the fungus, making it more difficult to control in the future.

Biological controls,

such as the use of beneficial microorganisms, can also be effective in managing Botrytis blight. These microorganisms, such as Trichoderma spp., can compete with the fungus for nutrients and space, reducing its ability to infect the plant.

Conclusion

Botrytis blight is a serious disease that can have a significant impact on the quality and quantity of roses produced. The disease is caused by the fungus Botrytis cinerea, which thrives in cool and moist conditions. Management of Botrytis blight involves a combination of cultural practices, chemical treatments, and biological controls. Good sanitation practices, such as cleaning tools and equipment, and proper plant spacing can help prevent the disease from spreading. When chemical treatments are necessary, they should be used judiciously to prevent the development of resistance in the fungus. Biological controls, such as the use of beneficial microorganisms, can also be effective in managing the disease. By employing a combination of these strategies, rose growers can effectively manage Botrytis blight and ensure the health and vitality of their plants.

Rose Rosette Disease

Rose Rosette disease is caused by a virus known as the Rose Rosette virus (RRV). It is spread by a tiny eriophyid mite known as the Phyllocoptes fructiphilus. The mite feeds on the rose plant, transmitting the virus in the process.

One of the most distinctive symptoms of Rose Rosette disease is the abnormal growth of the plant. Infected plants may produce clusters of thin, spindly stems, known as witches' brooms. These growths are characterized by an abundance of small, thin branches, which give the plant a bushy, unkempt appearance. The leaves on the witches' brooms are smaller and paler than those on the healthy parts of the plant, and they may also be distorted or twisted.

In addition to witches' brooms, Rose Rosette disease can cause other symptoms, including excessive thorniness, reddening of the leaves, and premature leaf drop. Infected plants may also have stunted growth, reduced vigor, and reduced flower production.

Causes

As mentioned, Rose Rosette disease is caused by a virus called the Rose Rosette virus. The virus is transmitted by the Phyllocoptes fructiphilus mite, which is believed to be the only vector for the disease. The mite is very small, measuring only about 0.2 mm in length, and can be difficult to detect.

Rose Rosette disease is most commonly found in North America, where it is a significant problem for rose growers. However, it has also been reported in Europe, Asia, and Australia. The disease affects all types of roses, including shrub roses, hybrid tea roses, and climbing roses.

Management Strategies

Unfortunately, there is no cure for Rose Rosette disease. Infected plants must be removed and destroyed to prevent the virus from spreading to other plants. If left untreated, the disease can spread rapidly, and infected plants can die within a few years.

To prevent the spread of Rose Rosette disease, it is essential to maintain good sanitation practices. Infected plants should be removed as soon as they are identified, and all plant debris should be carefully disposed of to prevent the mites from spreading. It is also important to avoid planting roses too close together, as this can increase the likelihood of the disease spreading.

In addition to sanitation practices, there are some other management strategies that can help to reduce the impact of Rose Rosette disease. These include:

1. Using resistant varieties: Some rose varieties are more resistant to Rose Rosette disease than others. By planting resistant varieties, growers can reduce the likelihood of the disease occurring.

2. Pruning: Regular pruning can help to remove any infected plant material before the disease can spread. Infected branches should be removed, and the pruning shears should be disinfected between cuts to prevent the spread of the virus.

3. Insecticides: Insecticides can be used to control the mites that spread Rose Rosette disease. However, it is important to use insecticides carefully and according to the label instructions to prevent harm to beneficial insects and other non-target organisms.

4. Monitoring: Regular monitoring can help to detect the early signs of Rose Rosette disease. Infected plants should be removed as soon as they are identified to prevent the disease from spreading.

Conclusion

Rose Rosette disease is a devastating disease that can quickly kill infected plants. It is caused by a virus transmitted by the Phyllocoptes fructiphilus mite and is characterized by witches' brooms, stunted growth, and premature leaf drop. Unfortunately, there is no cure for Rose Rosette disease, and infected plants must be removed and destroyed to prevent the virus from spreading. To prevent the disease, it is essential to maintain good sanitation practices, use resistant varieties, prune regularly, and monitor plants for early signs of infection.

Rose Rosette disease is a significant problem for rose growers in North America and has also been reported in other parts of the world. As such, ongoing research is being conducted to develop effective management strategies for the disease. In the meantime, it is essential for rose growers to remain vigilant and take steps to prevent the spread of the disease to protect their plants and the wider rose-growing community.

CHAPTER 12 THE TOP 5 WORST PESTS FOR ROSES

Roses are one of the most popular and beloved flowering plants in the world. Known for their beauty, fragrance, and versatility, roses are grown in gardens, landscapes, and as cut flowers. However, roses are also susceptible to various pests that can cause significant damage to their growth and development. In this essay, we will discuss the five worst pests for roses, their characteristics, the damage they cause, and methods for their control.

Aphids

Rose aphids (Macrosiphum rosae) are a significant pest of rose plants worldwide. These tiny insects, also known as greenfly, feed on the sap of the plant, causing wilting, distortion, and even death of the plant. The economic importance of rose aphids is significant, as rose plants are cultivated for their ornamental value and are a high-value commodity in the floral industry. This

essay aims to provide an overview of rose aphids, including their biology, distribution, and management strategies.

Biology

Rose aphids are small, soft-bodied insects belonging to the order Hemiptera and family Aphididae. They measure approximately 2mm in length and can be either green or pink in color. Rose aphids have a relatively short life cycle, with the nymphal stage lasting approximately seven days, and the adult stage lasting up to four weeks. Female aphids reproduce parthenogenetically, meaning that they do not require a male partner to produce offspring. One female aphid can produce up to 80 offspring in a single season, making them a prolific pest.

Rose aphids feed on the sap of the plant using their piercing-sucking mouthparts. The damage caused by their feeding can cause leaves to become yellow and wilted, stems to become distorted, and flowers to fail to open properly. Aphids also secrete a sticky, sugary substance known as honeydew, which can attract other pests such as ants and promote the growth of black sooty mold.

Distribution

Rose aphids are native to Europe, but they have since been introduced to other parts of the world, including North America, Asia, and Australia. They are most commonly found on cultivated roses but can also infest other plants in the Rosaceae family, such as apples, pears, and strawberries. In some areas, rose aphids have become a significant pest of wild roses, causing damage to natural ecosystems.

Management Strategies

The management of rose aphids involves both cultural and chemical control methods. Cultural control involves the use of practices that make the plant less attractive to aphids, such as planting roses in areas that receive plenty of sunlight and good air circulation. Removing weeds and dead plant material can also help to reduce the likelihood of aphids infesting the plant. Additionally, natural predators such as ladybugs and lacewings can be introduced to the area to feed on the aphids.

Chemical control

involves the use of insecticides to kill the aphids. However, the use of pesticides can have adverse effects on the environment, including harm to beneficial insects, such as bees and butterflies. As such, it is essential to use pesticides judiciously and follow all label instructions carefully. Additionally, it is recommended to rotate between different insecticides to reduce the likelihood of the aphids developing resistance.

Another management strategy is the use of biological control methods, such as the introduction of parasitoids or predators. Parasitoids are insects that lay their eggs inside the body of the aphids, killing them in the process. The most commonly used parasitoids for controlling rose aphids are Aphidius colemani and Aphidius ervi. Predators, such as lacewings and ladybugs, can also be used to control aphid populations. These predators feed on the aphids, preventing them from reproducing and causing damage to the plant.

In conclusion, rose aphids are a significant pest of rose plants worldwide. Their biology and life cycle make them a prolific pest, and their feeding can cause significant damage to the plant. The management of rose aphids involves a combination of cultural, chemical, and biological control methods. It is essential to use these methods judiciously to reduce the likelihood of adverse effects on the environment and to rotate between different control

In conclusion, rose aphids are a significant pest of rose plants worldwide. Their biology and life cycle make them a prolific pest, and their feeding can cause significant damage to the plant. The management of rose aphids involves a combination of cultural, chemical, and biological control methods. It is essential to use these methods judiciously to reduce the likelihood of adverse effects on the environment and to rotate between different control methods to prevent the aphids from developing resistance. The use of natural predators and parasitoids for biological control is an effective and environmentally friendly approach that can be used in conjunction with other management methods.

As the ornamental value of rose plants continues to increase, the importance of managing rose aphids becomes more significant. Researchers and growers continue to explore new and innovative methods for controlling rose aphids while minimizing their impact on the environment. The development of new technologies and approaches will undoubtedly play a crucial role in the management of rose aphids in the future.

Overall, the management of rose aphids requires a multifaceted approach that involves a combination of cultural, chemical, and biological control methods. The success of these methods relies on the judicious use of insecticides, the introduction of natural predators and parasitoids, and the implementation of cultural practices that make the plant less attractive to aphids. By using these strategies in conjunction with one another, growers can effectively manage rose aphids and minimize their impact on the plant and the environment.

Spider Mites

Spider mites are one of the most common pests found in rose gardens. These tiny arachnids can cause significant damage to rose bushes, resulting in stunted growth, leaf discoloration, and decreased flower production. Understanding the biology and behavior of rose spider mites is crucial for effective pest management in rose gardens. In this essay, we will discuss the taxonomy, biology, behavior, and management of rose spider mites.

Taxonomy

Rose spider mites belong to the family Tetranychidae, which includes over 1,200 species of spider mites. They are also known as two-spotted spider mites or red spider mites, depending on their coloration. The scientific name of the rose spider mite is Tetranychus urticae Koch.

Biology

Rose spider mites are very small, measuring only about 0.5 mm in length. They are oval-shaped and have eight legs. Their coloration can vary from pale yellow to green or red, depending on their age and the stage of development. The adults have two dark spots on their bodies, which give rise to their common name, two-spotted spider mites.

Rose spider mites are prolific breeders, with females laying up to 20 eggs per day. The eggs are laid on the undersides of leaves and hatch within a few days. The immature stages of the spider mites, known as nymphs, resemble the adults but are smaller and lack the dark spots.

Rose spider mites feed on the sap of rose leaves, using their sharp mouthparts to pierce the plant tissue and suck out the juices. This feeding activity can cause damage to the leaves, resulting in discoloration and wilting. Severe infestations can lead to defoliation and stunted growth of the rose bushes.

Behavior

Rose spider mites are typically found on the undersides of leaves, where they are protected from predators and environmental stressors. They are more active in warm, dry weather conditions and can reproduce rapidly under these conditions.

Rose spider mites are known for their ability to spin webs, which can cover the undersides of leaves and form a protective barrier around the colony. These webs can also be used to travel from one leaf to another or to other plants in the vicinity.

Management

Effective management of rose spider mites involves a combination of cultural, mechanical, and chemical control measures. Cultural control measures include maintaining healthy plants through proper irrigation and fertilization practices. Removing infested leaves and debris from the garden can also reduce the population of spider mites.

Mechanical control measures involve physically removing spider mites from the plants. This can be done using a strong jet of water, which can dislodge the mites from the leaves. Sticky traps and yellow sticky cards can also be used to capture the spider mites.

Chemical control measures involve the use of insecticides to kill the spider mites. However, care must be taken when using insecticides, as they can also harm beneficial insects and pollinators. It is important to follow label instructions and use insecticides only as a last resort.

Biological control measures involve the use of natural enemies to control the population of spider mites. Predatory mites, such as Phytoseiulus persimilis, are effective in controlling spider mite populations. Ladybugs and lacewings are also natural enemies of spider mites and can be introduced into the garden to help control the population.

Rose spider mites are a common pest in rose gardens, and their feeding activity can cause significant damage to rose bushes. Understanding the biology and behavior of these pests is crucial for effective pest management. Cultural, mechanical, chemical, and biological control measures can be used to manage spider mite populations

Japanese Beetles

Japanese beetles (Popillia japonica) are a notorious pest in the United States. These beetles were first discovered in New Jersey in 1916, and since then, they have spread across the country, causing significant damage to crops, flowers, and ornamental plants. In this essay, we will explore the history, biology, behavior, and control of Japanese beetles, using academic-style writing.

History of Japanese Beetles in the United States

Japanese beetles are native to Japan, where they are not considered a significant pest due to the presence of natural predators and parasites. However, in the early 20th century, these beetles were accidentally introduced to the United States through the shipment of Japanese iris bulbs. The first documented sighting of Japanese beetles in the US was in New Jersey in 1916, and by the 1930s, they had spread to the Midwest and the South.

One reason for the rapid spread of Japanese beetles in the US is their ability to adapt to a wide range of environments and hosts. These beetles feed on more than 300 species of plants, including turfgrass, corn, soybeans, roses, and fruit trees. They also have a high reproductive rate, with females laying up to 60 eggs during their 4-6 week lifespan.

Biology and Behavior of Japanese Beetles

J   apanese beetles are small, metallic green beetles with copper-colored wings. They are about half an inch long and have six small white tufts of hair along their abdomen. Adult beetles emerge from the soil in late May or early June and feed on the leaves, flowers, and fruits of plants during the day. They are particularly attracted to plants with high levels of nitrogen and prefer to feed in sunny areas.

Japanese beetles are not particularly fast flyers, but they can travel up to 5 miles from their original location in search of food and mates. They also emit pheromones to attract other beetles, leading to large congregations on plants. These congregations can cause significant damage to plants, as the beetles skeletonize leaves, leaving only the veins intact.

In addition to feeding on plants, Japanese beetles also mate and lay eggs in the soil. Females typically lay their eggs in clusters of 2-5 in the soil near the roots of grasses and other plants. The eggs hatch in 2-3 weeks, and the larvae feed on the roots of grasses and other plants for 10 months before pupating in the soil. The following spring, the adult beetles emerge from the soil and begin the cycle again.

Control of Japanese Beetles

Controlling Japanese beetles is a challenging task, as they have few natural predators in the United States. Chemical pesticides are commonly used to control adult beetles and larvae, but these can have negative impacts on the environment and other beneficial insects. Additionally, repeated use of pesticides can lead to the development of resistance in Japanese beetles.

One alternative to chemical pesticides is the use of pheromone traps. These traps contain a lure that attracts male beetles, which are then trapped inside the device. However, pheromone traps have been found to attract more beetles than they capture, leading to increased damage to nearby plants.

Another method of controlling Japanese beetles is the use of cultural practices, such as handpicking and pruning. Handpicking involves manually removing adult beetles from plants and dropping them into a bucket of soapy water, which kills them. Pruning involves removing damaged plant parts and encouraging plant growth to compensate for the loss of leaves and branches.

Thrips

Rose thrips are tiny insects that feed on roses and other plants, causing damage to the leaves and flowers. They belong to the order Thysanoptera, which includes over 6,000 species worldwide. Rose thrips are one of the most common pests of roses, and they can be difficult to control. This essay will provide an overview of rose thrips, including their life cycle, behavior, and impact on roses. It will also discuss the different methods of controlling these pests.

Life Cycle of Rose Thrips

Rose thrips go through a complete metamorphosis, consisting of four stages: egg, larva, pupa, and adult. The female thrips lay their eggs inside the rose buds or in the crevices of the bark on the stems. The eggs are oval and about 0.2 mm in length. The eggs hatch into larvae within five to seven days, and the larvae begin to feed on the leaves and flowers of the rose plant. The larvae are very small, only about 1 mm in length, and they are pale yellow or green in color.

After a few days of feeding, the larvae drop to the ground and burrow into the soil to pupate. The pupal stage lasts for approximately two weeks, after which the adult thrips emerge. The adult thrips are tiny, only about 1.5 mm in length, and they are slender and dark in color. The adult female thrips can lay up to 60 eggs during their lifespan, which is usually two to three weeks.

Behavior of Rose Thrips

Rose thrips are very mobile and can move quickly between plants. They are most active during warm, dry weather, and they tend to feed on new growth and flowers. They are attracted to the colors blue and yellow, which is why sticky traps of these colors are often used to monitor their presence. Rose thrips feed by puncturing the surface of the plant and sucking out the sap. This can cause damage to the leaves and flowers, resulting in a silvery or bronzed appearance. The damaged leaves may also curl, distort, or drop prematurely.

Impact of Rose Thrips on Roses

Rose thrips can cause significant damage to roses, both aesthetically and economically. The feeding damage can result in a loss of vigor and reduced growth, as well as a decrease in flower production and quality. The damage can also make the roses more susceptible to diseases and other pests. In addition, the damage caused by rose thrips can reduce the value of cut roses for sale in the floral industry.

Control of Rose Thrips

There are several methods of controlling rose thrips, including cultural, chemical, and biological control.

Cultural Control

Cultural control involves practices that reduce the likelihood of rose thrips infestations. These practices include:

- Planting rose varieties that are resistant to thrips
- Pruning and removing infested plant material
- Providing proper nutrition and watering to promote plant health
- Using mulch to reduce soil moisture and discourage thrips from pupating in the soil
- Keeping the garden free of weeds and debris, which can harbor thrips and other pests.

Chemical Control

Chemical control involves the use of pesticides to kill or repel rose thrips. There are several types of pesticides that can be used to control thrips, including insecticidal soaps, pyrethroids, and neonicotinoids. However, the use of pesticides can have negative effects on the environment, including harm to non-target species and the development of pesticide resistance in thrips populations. Therefore, it is important to use pesticides judiciously and follow all label instructions.

Biological Control

Biological control involves the use of natural enemies to control rose thrips populations.

Biological control involves the use of natural enemies to control rose thrips populations. One of the most effective natural enemies of rose thrips is the predatory mite, Amblyseius cucumeris. These mites feed on the eggs and larvae of thrips and can significantly reduce thrips populations. Other natural enemies include lacewings, ladybugs, and parasitic wasps.

In addition, the use of beneficial nematodes can be effective in controlling thrips in the soil. These nematodes feed on the pupal stage of thrips in the soil, preventing them from emerging as adults.

Integrated Pest Management (IPM) is a holistic approach to pest management that combines cultural, chemical, and biological control methods to manage pests in an environmentally sustainable way. IPM involves monitoring pest populations, identifying the pest species and their life cycle, and using appropriate control methods at the right time.

IPM can be an effective approach to managing rose thrips, as it allows for the use of non-chemical control methods and reduces the reliance on pesticides. In addition, IPM can help prevent the development of pesticide resistance in thrips populations.

Conclusion

Rose thrips are a common pest of roses and can cause significant damage to the plants. They go through a complete metamorphosis, consisting of egg, larva, pupa, and adult stages, and are attracted to the colors blue and yellow. Cultural, chemical, and biological control methods can be used to manage thrips populations, and IPM is an effective approach to pest management that combines these methods in a sustainable way. By understanding the behavior and life cycle of rose thrips and using appropriate control methods, it is possible to manage thrips populations and protect rose plants from damag

Rose Chafers

Rose chafers are tan or green beetles that feed on the flowers, leaves, and buds of rose plants. They are most active during the summer months and can cause significant damage to the plant. Rose chafers can skeletonize the plant by chewing irregular holes in the leaves. In addition, they can cause damage to the flowers by feeding on the petals.

Controlling rose chafers on roses can be challenging. One method is to manually remove the beetles from the plant by handpicking them or using a vacuum. Another method is to apply insecticides specifically designed to control rose chafers. It is important to note that insecticides can harm beneficial insects and pollinators, so their use should be limited.

Roses are susceptible to various pests that can cause significant damage to their growth and development. The five worst pests for roses are aphids, spider mites, Japanese beetles, thrips, and rose chafers. These pests can cause distortion of new growth, yellowing of leaves, stunted growth, premature leaf drop, and damage to flowers. Controlling these pests on roses can be challenging, and there are both natural and chemical control options available. It is important to use these control methods judiciously to minimize harm to beneficial insects and pollinators. By properly managing these pests, rose plants can thrive and continue to provide beauty and enjoyment for years to come.

CHAPTER 12 FINAL CONCLUSION

Rose propagation is a complex and intricate process that requires careful attention to detail and a thorough understanding of the biological mechanisms that underlie plant growth and development. In this study, we have explored the different methods of rose propagation, including stem cuttings, layering, grafting, and budding, and have discussed the advantages and disadvantages of each method.

Stem cuttings are the most commonly used method of rose propagation and are relatively easy to perform. They involve taking a cutting from a healthy parent plant and rooting it in soil or water. While this method is simple and cost-effective, it can take several months for the cutting to develop roots and establish itself as a new plant.

Layering involves bending a low-lying stem of a parent plant into the soil and allowing it to develop roots before separating it from the parent plant. This method is useful for producing larger, more mature plants quickly and can be used to propagate a variety of different rose species.

Grafting and budding are more complex methods of rose propagation that involve joining the stem or bud of one plant onto the rootstock of another. These methods require a high degree of skill and precision but can produce plants with desirable characteristics that are not present in the parent plant.

Overall, the success of rose propagation depends on a number of factors, including the type of rose being propagated, the method used, and the environmental conditions in which the plant is grown. It is important to choose the most appropriate method of propagation for each individual plant and to provide optimal growing conditions to ensure the best chance of success.

In conclusion, rose propagation is a fascinating and important area of plant science that has been studied and practiced for centuries. While there is no one-size-fits-all approach to rose propagation, understanding the different methods and factors that influence success can help growers produce healthy, robust plants with desirable characteristics. Further research in this area may lead to the development of new and improved methods of propagation, as well as a deeper understanding of the biological mechanisms that govern plant growth and development.

117

Printed in Poland
by Amazon Fulfillment
Poland Sp. z o.o., Wrocław

24659919R00067